Turkish Delight, Montreal Winter

poems

Sonia Saikaley

TSAR

We acknowledge the support of the Canada Council for the Arts for our publishing program. We also acknowledge support from the Government of Ontario through the Ontario Arts Council.

We acknowledge the financial support of the Government of Canada through the Canada Book Fund for our publishing activities

Canada Council for the Arts Conseil des Arts du Canada ONTARIO ARTS COUNCIL CONSEIL DES ARTS DE L'ONTARIO Canada

Cover design by Peggy Stockdale
Cover photograph by Goran Petkovski
Author photograph by Nora Nesrallah

Saikaley, Sonia
Turkish delight, Montreal winter : poems / Sonia Saikaley.

ISBN 978-1-894770-97-2

I. Title.

PS8637.A4495T87 2012 C811'.6 C2012-905391-0

Printed and bound in Canada by Coach House Printing

TSAR Publications
P. O. Box 6996, Station A
Toronto, Ontario M5W 1X7
Canada

www.tsarbooks.com

For my sisters, my fellow musketeers

Contents

From the Roots of an Olive Tree

Conception

In a mountain village along the Mediterranean Sea
he sat in the dry field, eating
eating a feast of olives and pita bread.

Later under a deep ochre sky
his lover's limbs entwined with his
on the earth of the olive grove
lips tasted flesh
that smelled of earth and olive trees
as fingers traced desire
along bellies pressed
together

the seed grew in the woman's belly;
the roots of the olive reached across seas.

Forthright in a Foreign Country

Dearest love, he wrote

on a postcard
of the Parliament buildings.
This country is vaster than I imagined.
People of all races and colours live and breathe in peace.
This country is where we can live and love
each other. I await your arrival.
May the Red Sea guide you into the Mediterranean;
its current pushes you safely into the Atlantic and
towards the harbour of my soul.

With a thousand kisses,
your expatriate love.

A Cauldron of Women's Rights

A slap across her face
punches to her swollen belly
tiny kicks under her ribs—
the baby is still alive, she sighs . . .

fetus in her womb
lurches to its grandfather's anger

letters and postcards from Canada
scattered on the floor, torn pieces
of a discovered love affair.

She is pregnant and unwed.

Her papa grabs her by the hair,
pushes her face into a pot of boiling water.

All in a Day's Work

The surgeon at the hospital
scrapes and scrapes burned flesh
sweat drips from his forehead
latex gloves stick to fingers

that sculpt what flesh remains

Can you believe the woman's father is a judge?

Justice is blind but this bastard had open eyes
the entire time he held his daughter's
head down

His colleague sighs—
his tongue numb . . .
steel tongs in unsteady hands;
he hates this part of the job,
delivering a dead baby.

The Request

1\.
Dearest love,

it has been a few months.
Not one letter, nor phone call.
I have tried several times, the static
of long distance lines is all I hear.
Your voice is a memory
of your face. Please write
soon and send me a photograph
before I forget your dark almond eyes, lovely smile.

Yours forever.

2\.
Dearest love,

it has been a year since I heard from you.
Perhaps you found another . . .
Send a wire, a note, a lipstick kiss
anything
to let me know you still love me.

Sadly missing you.

3\.
Dear One,

I suppose your heart and mind
no longer entwined
with mine.
You are in love with another.
Yours truly.

Poetic Hallucinations

In the cell
she rocks and clutches a blanket in her arms
sings an old lullaby before the next shot
pulsates through swollen veins.

Her mind belongs to the drugs
the nurses force into
dark purplish-blue veins

she drifts to a place
where olive trees grow

her lover presses
sensuous words into her flesh;
she trembles and sighs
falling into his urgent embraces.

The Last Letter

One day at the asylum in a city among ruins,
a strange package arrives
for the disfigured woman in 3B

an urn handcrafted by a Cree artist
"Made in Canada" stamped on the bottom

a kind nurse opens the cream-coloured envelope
reads out the contents for the patient

My soul always belonged to you.
Perhaps I am back in the olive grove.
I always loved tending those trees!
You know, love, I married you in my dreams.

Tears roll down
folds of scarred, wrinkled flesh

he still loved me
after all these years, her old voice shaking

her eyes stare past the nurse's shoulders
out the barb-wired window
the cedars in the distance
dance with sun, touch
tips of snow-covered mountains

a lifetime ago
warm bodies embraced
        in the company of olive trees . . .

My Father's Homeland

An Evening Meal

One evening with the wind shouting
like a drunken man,
my father walked into the house
hot breath pressed against
the back of my mother's neck.
She turned around, touched his cheek.
Her caress warmed cold flesh.
"Jim," she said, "you're shivering."
They clung together
warmth spreading from skin to skin.

My father planted olive trees
nurtured each one,
his children.
His skin darkened by the bright sun.
On the horizon, the sun's rays yellowed
pale blue skies.
His family owned
sheep too, not just trees.

His uncle fed the sheep,
sheared their wool;
they danced in his large hands.

My father could never be their keeper.
To be a good shepherd,
you mustn't grow attached to the sheep.
He'd see their eyes, hear their voices in his dreams.
Everyone knows, even a young child:
livestock eventually become dinner
served with a side plate of potatoes.

The Sounds

The sound of slaughter
awoke my father
most mornings in the mountain village
he longed for
when Canadian winters
shivered old bones.

The sound of lambs crying
fills his eardrums;
their shrieks travel over hillsides
of his village, over oceans dividing
his chosen home and birth country.
The sheep cry, waking him.

He sits up and glances at the
photograph of his brother;
old and torn
from a turbulent sea
voyage from there to here.
He remembers
seamen shouting for order
rats biting passengers' ankles.
The photo of his dead brother
clutched in his hands.

Grasping Death

Tony was two years younger than Jim.
He dreamt of being a soldier
like the ones surrounding the border.
Machine guns echoed into the sky.
Tony dreamt of wearing the brown uniform,
a gun close to his chest.
One day, he found one in a field
an eight-year old boy with a pretend gun.
Tony aimed and fired
the barrel pointed in the direction
of his heart, the bullet pierced his skin, bones.
Awoken by the sound of slaughter,
Jim ran outside and fell to his knees
beside his brother.

He held onto Tony, rocking back and forth
his brother's heart exploded
into his palms.

My Father's Homeland

1.
I hold my father's hands in my own.
They are now small from old age
from the tumours living in his body.
I want to be buried next to my brother, he says.
In the village where
beauty is painted
on the blurred background of war.
Where springs flow freely
the sun shines brightly
gunshots pound.
Take me home, my father says.
I weep and nod in agreement.

2.
My first visit to my parents' birthplace.
A language I speak with uncertainty
plays like music as I push my father
out of the airport to my cousin's car.
We greet each other with
one kiss on each cheek.
My cousin bends down,
kisses my father in the same manner.

Nights are cool here
a glimpse of white frost
on hilltops
My father curses Canadian winters.

Now he sleeps soundly.
Plagued with insomnia,
my stomach churns with homesickness.

I meet cousins for the first time.
Rita, Samira, Michel, Yussef, Josephine

the list goes on
a family tree
roots as long as the Rideau Canal.

3.
I have learned the ways of this country.
This mysterious place
my father calls home.
I look like everyone else,
but sound different.
Here, I am the one with the accent.
A foreigner despite sharing
the same last name.

One evening
my cousins drink *ahweh* heartily.
I choke on its bitterness.
Here, cousin, put some sugar in it, Rita says.
I look at my father across from me.
He smiles, takes my face into his hands,
softly touches my cheeks.

That night,
my father dies.
I fulfill his wish
place wild flowers on his grave
next to his brother.

A Recurring Theme

He draws the stomach,
or whatever remains of it, with ease.

In all his studies,
the charts and dissections
colourful maps of the human body
he learned a thing or two about sketching
without formal art training.

An audience studies his sketch
as if he were Diego Rivera
creating a public mural.

The artist exclaims:
It's come back. It's come back.

Tears do not fall, this time;
my body numb.

This is a private matter—
the primary colour on the artist's palette
surrounded by his offspring.

In other circumstances,
I may have thought him
an extraordinary artist.

I look at my father's face,
nerves twitch around his mouth.

The skilled surgeon
darkens the looming death.

Perhaps in a gallery in Mexico City,
sipping rose-coloured wine
I may have praised his talent.

The Prodigal Daughter

As my father lies dying in a hospital room,
I smell the antiseptic in the air
hear the sound of the monitor
his shallow breath.

I am the disobedient daughter
by his bedside,
gripping his hand.
Jaundice stains his skin.
I lean in, bury my head in the hollow hole
where his belly used to be.

His body is a war field
and I the soldier gone AWOL
returned.

I grasp his thin hand and cry.
Between short, quick breaths
there is silence. I yearn for him to speak
Morphine has axed the willow tree
over the river of mourning.

I listen to his breath,
each one a struggle
and remember how we fought
for the final word
in every argument.

Soldier

You fought in a war against
an enemy stationed in your own body.

You negotiated with
chemotherapy, morphine.
Even tried herbs,
sucked grapes
baptized in holy water.
A pilgrimage to the local cathedral.
Your lips touched
the Bishop's hand.

Tumours still invaded your skin.
You drank
from the goblet of death.

In a vineyard in the Beqaa Valley
              spoiled wine dripped
from a barrel of crushed grapes
into your dark blue veins.

Father's Day

They unwrap the gifts:
cologne, socks, shirts
wrapped in blue tissue paper.

My father smiles peacefully.

Tears slip down cheeks
We wear our grief
in black clothes.

Others celebrate Father's Day with
scrambled eggs, sausages, pancakes
dripping with blueberries and Maple syrup,
a swim in the lake at the cottage or
the entire family crammed in a pew,
elbows touching, shoulders brushing,
listening to a church mass.

We celebrate with a wake.

My sisters and I cry:
Happy Father's Day, Babba!
We crowd around him,
our bodies pressing against
the mahogany casket.

I rest my lips
on his forehead.
The frigid flesh reminds me
of a winter's day.
But it is June
the parlour is hot.

I fall back into the chair

stare past shoulders
of relatives and friends.

My father smiles peacefully.

A Daughter Remembers

You swore under your breath.
I wondered, Did you curse God
for providing you only with daughters?

I lifted you out of the bathtub.
Your body shook,
you lowered your head
ashamed I had to view
your nakedness so openly.
Tears mixed with soapy water.

Skin hung loose
on feeble bones.

A child's body now.

What's the matter, Babba?
The towel absorbs a rivulet of dewdrops.
The water wrinkled my old skin even more.
I look like a dried-out prune, you laughed weakly.

You rested your
hand on my cheek,
the steam of the bath
rising like early morning fog.
Thank you.

6:15 AM
a Saturday morning
in June. I remember the rain,
the damp smell of it in my hair as I ran
into the hospital, into your room.

I missed you
by five minutes.

The weeks following your death,
the memories of your illness still vivid:
    sallow skin,
    ankles as thin as my wrists,
    the suffering you endured.

I tossed and turned
in restless sleep.

Memories ripen slowly
like grapes in a vineyard.

Now I remember other things.

The Return

Remember me, you cried.

I wept and my tears
washed your blistered feet.
The sodden ground absorbed footprints and memory.

I clutch a black and white photograph:
you pose in front of the Temple of Jupiter.
Performers dance between pillars in the background.
The town of Baalbeck thrives
with Fairouz in an apricot silk gown singing
amongst Roman ruins.

I close my eyes and imagine
the mountain village you were born in
whispering through the wind, *Come, come.*

Years ago you stood on a ship's deck
with your head bowed, a suitcase in one hand.
You mouthed the word goodbye, swallowed hard,
and watched a rat scurry through a broken plank.
Now you return,

falling into her arms
you taste saltwater at the corners of your mouth

you accept offerings of *arak,* baklava,
even have the strength to dance,
laugh, exchange pleasantries.

Gravel paths cover your blue leather shoes;
dirt sticks to flesh as you walk on

a stretch of road like the *Via Dolorosa.*
Still shadowed by illness
your skin resembles ancient yellow robes.

To Decipher a Bomb

Through Silence

The dead are great listeners.
I speak soliloquies—
they never interrupt.

I find solace
when the silver of the moon
paints each tombstone.

Shadows dance together
strangers introduced by death.

Inhibitions do not exist here.

I find solace
trace headstones
with tips of fingers
each letter, each name.
The dead alive as their names.

Their names strong, indestructible.

Sweet, Sweet Morpheus

Rippling waves
underground caves
ancient places of burial

Cancer bellows in cells
dormant now
pulsating with poison

Blood vessels swollen
fallen strands on sterile pillowcases

White, spotless walls
petals on the side table
wilted flowers in a porcelain vase

Visiting hours over for the day
Please stay, you mouth

A dam of flesh and bones
cracks and breaks
hurrying cascades down sunken cheeks

A scheduled visit from the god of sleep
in the form of bitter, crystalline

A volcano erupts
in a valley of bedpans and morphine

The Unexpected Visitor

His boxer shorts
dangle from a brass handle.
A cotton undershirt
on the dirty floor.

Jasmine soap
razor blades
still covered with stubble.

She used to lecture him
about his untidy habits.

A bathtub
lined with crimson stains
bleach cannot remove.

She can't bring herself
to pick them up,
nor mop the floor.

His blood still lives
between the cracks
of ceramic tiles.

The Hermit

They should have shipped him back
in a crate used to smuggle
ivory tusks of dead elephants.

All bones and yellow teeth,
skin no longer flesh but something else.
Clothes once clean
smell of gym socks and armpits.

The mission was meant to be peaceful.
He proudly wore the country's uniform.
Now he knows not where he belongs.

He wanders down alleys late at night
to avoid the light of day and people
in his gaze.

He searches for the things he lost: a wedding band,
a baseball glove
he gave his son.

A memory to be thrown away with Tuesday's trash
when the sun comes up.

His bronzed skin
a duffle bag
he carries.

Scars as deep as the Atlantic
swim on the surface of his body.
Between his collarbone and neck
exists undamaged skin.

Under a streetlight,
he pulls out a picture from his wallet,

studies his past.
His wife rests her head
in the nape of his neck.

A passerby looks in fright
as if a corpse
escaped the cemetery;
flesh eaten by maggots.

The man stuffs the photo
back into his wallet.

Shoulders hunched,
he drags himself
down the street
looking for moonlight.

The Undertaker's Wife

Your body smells of bleach
cold skin under my fingertips.

An unfamiliar lover might lose his way
along your curved hips.

My hands travel your body
with knowledge and expertise.
Decades of lovemaking
I memorized every birthmark, scar.

The lamp above
singes my forehead
salt tears and sweat
slide down hollow cheeks.

I stroke your face and
dress you in your Sunday's best.

In the Wake of a Lunar Eclipse

Most days, she sits
in the living room with photographs
planted between imported figurines
on the coffee table.

Crocuses grow in a garden
memories held in silver and
gold-trimmed frames.

She wears a new title
in black clothes:
the blouses, long skirts,
his old sweatshirts, trousers.

Love, you're my moon
and everything in between.

In the front garden
she falls to her knees
tending flowers
he planted a year ago,
clutches fistfuls of dirt
in her hands.

The Fortune Teller

She picks up the tiny teacup
reads cracked lines
of leftover Turkish coffee.

A gypsy, wanderer by trade
she travelled to Turkey, Syria, Lebanon
belly-danced in taverns,
then ended up in eastern Ontario.

But her wedding band bruised her finger.
She left her husband
with glacier winds swirling her hair,
phantom aromas of garlic, allspice, mint
lingered in dark strands
now silver,
she pulls at them and peers
into the cup again,
strains sunken eyes.

Once beautiful, village men sang
love ballads, strummed fingers on guitars
that later pressed into her olive skin.

Now old eyes look deep into the cup.
She leans forward,
elbows on table edge,
her wrinkled fingers entwine.
She tries to read her fate
but sees nothing,
only remnants of caffeine.

Climatic Memories

Black hair, olive skin
in the bedside frame.

My fingers push
the picture down
when entangled
in my lover's limbs.

Mama's serious, dark face
suffocated by my cherry oak dresser.

He groans,
You're not a child anymore
Why do you care what your mother thinks?

I close my eyes to
the space between her teeth
Like my own
shared DNA, made
different by choice.

I remember her rich, musical accent.

I wonder, *What were her dreams?*

Habibti, she says
A name no one calls
but my lover in translation:
honey, how does this feel?

Would she approve?
Sex outside of marriage
straining of two bodies
desperate to be one
clean sheets drenched with sweat.

I trace my lover's face
the beginnings of a beard
tickle my fingertips.
I bend down kiss each dark eyelid.

Fireflies

A chill blows into my pores
as if my flesh were an old cardigan
in the aftermath of moths.

You put your arms around me,
press your warm body against mine.
Now under the bed covers, the cold
a memory forgotten,
where one day, you'll be there too.

Your face, your scent, your touch
braided into the lobes of my brain:
the slant and pitch of your saying good morning,
the smell of strong Arabic coffee
you made for me every day.
The white powdery, Turkish delights
my tongue tasted on the corners of your lips,
fade slowly from my mind.

Tomorrow, you go back home
to the mountain village in the Beqaa Valley,
away from the cold,
where snow angels never surface in dry fields.

On this wintry day,
I swear I could see your kisses
if I stood outside naked,
your imprints on my skin would glow like fireflies
on a dark, moonless Arabian night.

On the Road to Beirut

Burning. Burning flesh.
The stench lodges in his brain.

These memories make him remember
his home near the delicate border,
where blue skies

explode in haunting visions, night sweats.
He prays for dementia, to make him forget,

the stone wall between East and West Beirut,
bullet holes lined up like beads

between aging fingers
click, clack, click, clack,
the prayer beads slide on the elastic string:
enamel taps enamel.

The dashboard of the minibus left a gash on his forehead.
Now too old to manoeuvre through narrow streets,
blood flows from his nose,
years after that day when a bomb shattered his life,
the lives of those travelling with him.

In another continent,
a country known for its glacier landscape,
he longs for a whole night's sleep
instead he remembers wiping blood with his sleeve,
the smell of burnt flesh and diesel
roads no longer roads, but crimson rivers
where dismembered limbs float beside him.

To Decipher a Bomb

A blood river from open wounds
gushes on a cobblestone path

civilians crucified by shards of blasted glass
several disfigured, deformed, burned

an effigy of innocents
amongst shells of missiles and bullets

the smell of bodily fluids mixes with hot air
dust soars, those alive

rub their eyes in disbelief

The Maternity Ward

In a hospital room, she lies in white sheets
her belly bandaged in gauze,
Her eyes stare vacantly out the window.

A squirrel scurries from branch to branch.
The year's first snowfall lands
in the creature's tail.

The room reeks of alcohol, mopped linoleum floors,
stale hospital food and the fresh scent of babies, the smooth skin.

She turns and gazes at the others in the room
newborns on their mothers' bellies,
proud husbands and grandparents.

Bouquets of flowers, potted plants,
balloons and stuffed animals on their tables
notes of sympathy, get well wishes,
epigraphs on her bedside
it'll be okay

She presses the small rod pinned on the hospital sheet
for the nurse to hurry.
A young woman in blue scrubs smiles "How can I help you?"

Her womb floats in a jar of formaldehyde,
preserved for medical students
the babies across from her cry.
She turns away, looks into the distance again.

The Arrival

Antarctic cold
chemotherapy-infested
bones

Jaundice spots
ovarian clots
belly swollen

She is barren

Her lover
frightened by her
frantic moans, groans, her
hip bones pushing into his

flees before coming.

Down There

Down There

Hands grip metal edges
naked under the hospital gown
she lies on the examining table

paper sheet crumples as
legs spread.

She stares at the ceiling
photographs of a tropical vacation
palm trees, seashells uncovered
in white sands.

She closes her eyes
remembers her childhood home:
the sea, mountains, goats,
dusty roads and fields.

She used to be a village girl
roaming the countryside
resisting dark-haired Samir, her beloved
in sheds, olive groves, riverbeds
his desire throbbing against her thighs.

Don't let anyone but your future husband
touch you down there,
her Babba warned.

The cold steel of the speculum
slowly enters her.
She winces, clenches her jaw,
sees Samir's bright face in the pictures
on the ceiling, his hands pushing up her skirt.

Now she lies still
until the doctor asks her
to open her legs wider.

The Wedding Sheet

On the hotel bed he spreads
a white sheet, fresh from
the laundry.

She can smell the detergent from
her chair in the corner
where she sits as if punished for speaking out
A schoolchild no more
she gazes out the window as
Niagara Falls tumble in the distance,
beams of light colour the dark sky.

He bends down, kisses her
the licorice taste of *arak*
in her mouth

She stares at her husband
black strands,
falling over his brow, as he leans
over the bed once more and
pushes tendrils away from deep-set eyes,
stands with hands on hips
as if inspecting the sheet for defects

No creases. And age
has not yellowed, made musty
scent of mothballs part of the cloth, or
the dry cleaner's bag
it was stuffed in, pressed and
passed into his hands by his mother

It is perfectly clean, white.
He smiles to himself
and undoes
his belt.

Something New, Something Blue

A new bride, Canadian born
the furrows begin to form.
She stares at the white sheet spread on the hotel bed
and concentrates, tries to remember
this custom, this passage in wedding magazines
flipped through.
Later, she lies in bed
her husband moves inside her
his elbows lean against the mattress.
She looks out the window again
the falls dawdling, the colourful lights die away,
her face tightens in his shadow.

She closes her eyes,
holds back the tears.

His hands clasp the sheet in place;
it wrinkles under her body,
her virginity
spills out

into folds of snow-white linen.

Family Honour

She is seen as clean,
a virgin, her parents think,
along with her future in-laws;
they smile from ear-to-ear.

Her mother-in-law places a white sheet
on the hotel bed, then
tiptoes down the hallway.

But on her wedding night,
when her husband enters
slowly and carefully
ruby drops don't flow down her thighs, or
on the snow-white linen.

She feels unclean in her silk lingerie,
lying underneath,
her secret buried in her womb,
unless her beloved husband speaks.
He is silent as he rolls over and falls asleep.

The festivities and wine make him forget
the crumpled cloth under her body.

She folds it up and
throws it down the laundry chute.

Another Season

They said she had childbearing hips,
the kind to push a child out
in a few short breaths
"You will make your husband proud," the old women clucked,
hens too old to hatch any more eggs
"Even prouder if the babies are boys."

But winters turned to springs, summers
to autumns, not one egg growing
only small clots gushing
into white linens, placed between her legs
she wrung them in calloused hands
on laundry days.

Her hands covered in soapsuds,
water falls from an old tap
into the washbasin.
She looks into the distance,

her husband walks in a grove,
shoulders droop, head bows,
studying the figs fallen
to the ground.

Later in each other's embrace, moonlight
whitewashes the walls of the small, stone house
breath hurrying, they shudder,
flesh glistening

She washes their lovemaking
from the bedding, rests her hands on her belly,
hoping his seed will grow in her womb.

Several weeks disappear
she visits the statue of Cybele;

weeps at the feet of the goddess
She looks up into her granite face, pleads
stumbling up the stone steps
droplets of blood trickle down her thighs.

She squeezes her soiled clothes,
turning the water pink.

Blessed Birth

I anoint your forehead with spring water
from a Tripoli fountain

I bottle some, place it in my overnight bag
water gushes down my thighs

I make the sign of the cross on your face
You do not flinch but smile

You could have been born in a stable
a saviour among peasants in a mountain village

But I forced myself onto a camel, travelled
through the ancient world

Fountains of the Divine Mother abounded on cobblestone
I bent down, bottle in hand, scooped blessed water

to anoint your forehead
thank Allah for this miracle: your birth

Foreigner's Etiquette

Silhouettes of olive branches darken
the pale walls in a tavern along the mountain

she sits with a glass of *arak,*
liquor, water and ice cubes mixed together

the only customer in this village restaurant
A belly dancer shakes her hips at the woman,

colourful beads jiggle around her waist;
the dancer drops a veil down the woman's back,

pulls it around her shoulders
It tickles the nape of her neck

she turns from the dancer's swinging breasts,
her cheeks redden as she looks down at her plate

the stuffed grape leaves, taboulleh, hommus
maza served before the roast leg of lamb

She doesn't know how to say
I don't eat meat in Arabic.

Harvesting Olives

Olive trees surround my childhood home
calloused hands shake boughs
sea green olives rain like hailstones.
Since my mother's death,
my father's skin furrows with each harvest.

Every year we send containers
by ship to distant cousins.
Tiny olives float in oil,
swirling through
a turbulent journey
from the Mediterranean to
the shores of the Canadian east coast.

I find a stray one lying on the ground and
grasp it between my fingers as if
memorizing its smoothness, colour.

I gaze back at the almost empty house,
the suitcase at the door,
then run through the olive grove,
past my father, spread my arms,
invite thrashing branches and scars
to remember the home I abandon
for broken English and snow.

Migration

The peace tower stands alone
silence tolls
in the old corridors
as I leave for the day

Outside
strung Christmas lights
shimmer rubies, emeralds and golds
on towering evergreens

In the indigo sky
fresh snowflakes
on my tongue
I hurry down the street to
my empty apartment

I stand alone in my kitchen
make dinner and think about my parents
in the mountain village

Icicles drip from steeped rooftops
as I abandon another workday
I look into the sky and watch
Canadian geese return in a symbol of peace,
a perfect v-shape
crocuses dusted with intricate snowflakes
the last before spring

The Longevity of Olives

The open suitcase tempts her
to fill its emptiness
her girlhood dream:
to leave this village

Let's go, throw in your clothes!

There are other signs too.
The steamship whistles in the Mediterranean
when she tosses and turns in restless sleep;
it hums a song for her.
Postcards from Canadian cousins
speak of a young country
where a lover awaits
her soul to be entwined with his
yearning for the new world;

but she hesitates, looks back,
an olive grove in her parents' field
her shepherd brother, sheep at his feet—
a messiah in modern clothes
A self-proclaimed bachelor
She would miss him, her parents.

This loss would maim her.

Her skin would sallow,
her dark curls turn silver and brittle.
Clotho, Lachesis, Atropos
turn their backs on her.
She'd shrivel, as
an olive.

Disintegration

1.
Dirty Arab!
The first time she heard these words,
she fled back to the house,
scrubbed her face

to erase the pigmentation.
She straightened her hair and coloured it
a rich golden of nectar and dreams.

2.
This course is to integrate
immigrants into Canadian society.

The language of the new world fills her days.
In the privacy of her kitchen she cooks
stuffed grape leaves, hommus, baba ghanouj
small dishes of maza.

On her lunch hours, she eats
cold cut sandwiches. She says a little prayer
makes the sign of the cross.

3.
Old roots buried in a side garden:
zucchini for the koosa
tomatoes for the taboulleh
green beans for the lubieh

Her hands plant
seeds in remembrance
Of fading memories.

What Immigration Officials Failed to Explain

In a side garden, squirrels
feast on her tomatoes.
She curses at them in Arabic;
the neighbours stare through closed blinds.

They say she is a gypsy, her skin
is olive, her hair is black
and curling; her hands move
when she speaks.

In the summer garden
leaves from the tomato stalk shrink
and the plants deteriorate, disappearing.
In September she walks into
a beauty salon. *Dye my hair*

and straighten the curls
she tells the hairdresser.

She learns to ask what she wants
without an accent.

The Visit

She stumbles up stone steps,
drops fresh petals
in the dust.
Her parents died
years ago.

She touches
her knee, a drop of crimson,
blood

from the same girl as
once lived in Kfarmichki,
a village of fig and olive trees.
Her hair is dyed and her clothes western.
She can barely speak her mother tongue.

You're still the same on the inside
said her shepherd brother.
He rests his calloused hands on her shoulders.
She turns from his gaze
back to the crypt.
A grey-stoned shack
a crucifix hangs above the entrance way.
A stranger
has visited their graves.

Turkish Delight, Montreal Winter

Shadows of stonewalled gardens and
limestone springs
A village girl sings

On this Arabian night
she takes flight
head wrapped in a silk scarf
the shackles of a strict
upbringing disintegrate

She runs through dry fields
of fig and olive trees
She sings in Arabic

She sails to the New World by ship
tripping over icy decks, glazed streets
She misses her Mama's delicious sweets:
baklawa, ma'moul, namura, Turkish delights
flavoured with rose water
Chai made with dry mint leaves

Her chest heaves
boots shuffle snowflakes
on Montreal's winding steps

Dusk till dawn
the rooster
on her parents' village farm
awakens her many, many miles away
in this land of glacier walkways

Speak English

You are born to a world of snow
so different from my village
I wrap you in swaddling cloth
tight as a parcel shipped from my womb

Months pass
you learn to call me *Mama*
You speak in my language:
hand gestures, smiles, fragmented words

The neighbours call you
a gypsy girl as you stumble
first steps on paved sidewalks

You stretch your arms out
into my embrace, you fall crying
your small mouth quakes

Years pass
you forget your mother tongue
words previously spoken
now broken
shards of Arabian nights
Turkish delights
once swallowed whole

I don't know you anymore, *habibti*
You shrug your shoulders and say,
Speak English

Strangers

The river in veins
connects us in the morning light.

Some time in the night
you squeeze between your father and me,
your hands press on my back.

I turn around,
open palms ready to play
Patty-cake, patty-cake, Baker's man
we whisper as your father sleeps.

Years before,
we shared the same body.
You swam in my woman's space,

backstroke, front stroke, doggy paddle
you tried them all, waking me most nights

But I never complained
You were a good baby.

Years pass and I do not know you
You are not the child I held to my bosom,

suckling breasts your tiny hands
grasp folds of flesh.

In western clothes you speak a language
difficult for me, raise your eyebrows
at my scarlet hip scarf.

You make eyes when my belly sways.

A scar forces remembrance

of my body harbouring your tiny body.

My hands cup your face, the way
they did years ago, you turn your head
my hands slip away

I hold them up to the light,
palms dried and cracked.

Lament

A mother speaks with uncertainty;
her speech broken.
A language never learned
for the country she resides in.
A home, where four daughters
flourished into young women.

Ancient bones under olive skin;
her downtown home
with grapevines
climbing along brick walls
reminds her of the small, stone house
in the Mediterranean where she was born.

The old woman sits on her porch
purple and red clouds the sky
She looks back on her life
and asks,

Did she live well?

The skin she inhabits
makes others wonder
Greek? Italian? Spanish?

Her olive skin, dark hair with silver
tossing in the early evening wind
speak her history.
Canadian, no one asks
on introduction.

Geese and Maple Trees

Freda sits in a park.
She lifts a book,
buries her eyes in printed words.

She doesn't see the woman at first
a shadow in the towering trees
moves closer to the bench
where Freda sits and reads.

Dirty bitch!

Words flung in the autumn air.

Leaves shake and fall,
land on Freda's shoulders.

She puts the book down
looks and sees the woman fast approaching
a bottle in her hand.

Dirty bitch!
Go back to your country—
You don't belong here!

Words flung in the autumn air.

Shards of glass
crash on the bench
inches away from Freda's face.

She gets up, shaking and
walks away from the crazy woman
with obscenities in her mouth.

You dirty Arab!
Go back home!

Passersby fumble with their bags
pretend not to see or hear

Words flung in the autumn air.

Freda closes her mouth, opens it,
closes it again.
She walks down the concrete street.

You don't belong here!

Words flung in the autumn air.

But she was born in this city
a place of geese and maples
not herds of sheep and olive trees.

Arabian Marketplace

Arabian Marketplace

She strolls through aisle upon aisle,
touches a blue charm:
to ward off the evil eye.

Marketplace by the sea.
Talkative vendors stand
behind cloth-draped tables.

Trinkets from the Middle East:
gold jewellery, waterpipes,
talismans of cedars

lost to embers,
hazy clouds of debris.

Sunlight sparkles on gold bangles,
a crucifix of Jesus Christ
on a woman's breast.

"How much for the stone?"

She barters with a vendor
in baggy trousers and
an apron with deep
pockets around his waist.

"Fifty thousand lira."
"Too much."
"For you, *habibti,* free."

Mother Mary

She stands in a pew
tilts her head, looks into the eyes
of the Virgin Mary, floating

on the domed ceiling.
The Mother gazes at the child
in the wooden seat.
A blue bead hangs on the woman's chain.

Head bowed, Mary sad
in the flicker of burning candles.

Light rain weeps
on the Church roof.

Allspice Feast

The smell of spiced ground beef
on skewers in a stone oven
puddings flavoured with rose water
salads sprinkled with dried mint leaves
engulf her as she leans on the counter, and

orders a maza of fattoush,
hommus, stuffed grape leaves.

She sits at a small table
Her eyes flit between her plate, the window.

Rain still falls, drenching vendors,
the man with baggy trousers
who gave her the blue charm.

She turns her head
meets the gaze of a young man sitting
across the table. He smiles.
She smiles shyly back, touches
the ring on her left finger.

She watches him get up, stand before her.

Without her permission, he sits down,
breaks a piece of pita bread
scoops up her leftover chickpeas.

"My name's Naji."
She tries not to stare at the food in his open mouth.

The Lunch Companion

"It all comes down to oil, really."

She shifts on the plastic chair,
nods her head politely
as Naji speaks about the politics of the Middle East.

He licks olive oil from his fingers.

He picks up a *zeitoun,* rolls it in his open palm.
Traces of garlic, herbs on calloused skin.
He pops it into his mouth, dislodges
the pit onto her empty plate.

"I have a plan that's explosive, you know," he says,
sinking deeper into his chair.

He now stands in khaki trousers,
a green cardigan,
pats his chest, pulls out
a wrinkled note of handwriting
unfolds it, folds it again,
stuffs it into his pocket.

She thinks, It's too warm for a sweater.

"Take my advice. You seem like a nice lady.
Get out before it's too late."

Wandering

Born and raised in the broken city of Beirut,
she's heard it all before.

No stranger needs to warn her, she thinks,
stepping outside once more.

The rain has stopped, sun sparkles
on the Mediterranean, waves brushing
concrete shore.

Mercedes zoom along busy streets,
swerving around pedestrians, other cars.

She walks through the marketplace
looks down at her wristwatch, tiny diamond
encased below the twelve.

Her husband was supposed to be here
an hour ago.

She hates it when he's late.

A Final Prayer

She catches a glimpse of a green sweater
a man hurrying, eyes narrowed,
underarm sweat stains.

Along the strip of Western stores,
she glances at her reflection.
High cheek-bones, thick hair
small furrows forming
around dark eyes.

The sky a pale blue,
light rays pour through
windowpanes.

"I warned you."

She raises her hands to her mouth
as glass breaks into kaleidoscopic pieces
and pierces her skin, crimson pours
on the cobblestone.

She falls to the earth and prays.

Reunited

"Don't be afraid, *habibti,*"
she hears her mother say.

Her mother's voice is now vivid again
It's been several years since she heard it.

She used to say this to her when she was a child,
too afraid to sleep in her own room
at her grandparents' village house.

She and her family lived in this old home
when the blistering Beirut heat
forced them to the mountains.

Her mother's been dead for years.

Now she hears her voice as if beside her,
feels her hand on hers,
her full lips brush against her forehead.

"Don't be afraid, *habibti*. You're home."

Premonition

He glances down at his wristwatch,
gold with a tiny diamond
below the number twelve,
a gift from his wife.

Back-to-back traffic
Sirens blast
ambulances swerve on cramped streets.

He taps his fingers against the steering wheel,
beats out a popular Lebanese song.
He promises to make it up to his wife,
take her to the finest restaurant,
buy her the best red wine,
ask the waiter to pour it

into a silver goblet.

He knows she hates it when he's late.

Casualty

A colossus of gunpowder
smothers the clear sky.
Embers on the red earth,
bodies trapped under bricks and stone.

A suicide bomber's farewell note
written in crimson ink.

Leather shoes on splayed feet.
A pile of rubble engulfs her.

Ashes slowly burn.
Sirens throb through broken cobblestone.
Rain descends

over her collarbone
a fine gold chain
glitters under washed-away dirt.

Acknowledgements

I would like to thank TSAR Publications, especially Nurjehan Aziz, for giving me a chance and for believing in my work. This publication would not have been possible without her generosity and support.

Some of these poems first appeared in online and print journals and I wish to thank the editors of those publications. My sincere thanks to Gillian Harding-Russell, who first suggested I put these poems in a collection. I am thankful to Susan Musgrave for her kindness and generous time in reading the manuscript.

Gratitude to my dear friends for their enthusiasm and support. I am grateful as ever for the friendship of Lynne McLeod, Darlene Miller, Susan Garden, Odelia Bay and Michelle Doody. I am blessed to have an amazing family and I thank them for their love and support. Many thanks to my niece Nora and her amazing photographic skills. Shukran to my mother for her inspiring and delicious Middle Eastern food. My gratitude to my late father and his beautiful and touching memories of his homeland.

Above all, thanks to my incredible sisters for their faith in me and my dreams.

Some of the poems in this collection were previously published as follows:

"To Decipher a Bomb" and "Fireflies" in *Illya's Honey,* Spring 2012.
"Through Silence" in *Blue Lake Review,* January 2012.
"The Return" and "The Sounds" in *Red River Review,* November 2011.
"The Fortune Teller" in *The Red Fez,* August 2011.
"The Visit" in *Every Day Poets* at www.everydaypoets.com, March 2011.
"The Last Letter" in *Burning Tree Press,* January 2011.
"The Wedding Sheet" and "Turkish Delight, Montreal Winter" in *Paragon* III, 2010.
"The Undertaker's Wife" in *Open Heart 4 Poetry Contest Anthology,* The Ontario Poetry Society, February 2010.
"On the Road to Beirut" in *[Word]: A Journal of Canadian Poetry,* 2010.
"The Hermit" in *Quills Canadian Poetry Magazine,* 2009.
"What Immigrant Officials Failed to Explain" in *Monday's Poem,* 2009.
"Another Season" in *Lavanderia: A Mixed Load of Women, Wash and Word,* 2009.
"My Father's Homeland" in *Inscribed,* March 2009.

"Down There" in *The Writer's Block* (Issue 1), December 2008.
"The Arrival" in *The Moose & Pussy* (Issue 2), Winter 2008/2009.
"Climatic Memories" in *Jones Av.* (Volume XII/2), Spring 2007.
"Foreigner's Etiquette" in *Blue Skies Poetry,* 2007.
"A Recurring Theme" in *Bywords Quarterly Journal* and Bywords.ca, 2006.
"The Unexpected Visitor" in *FreeFall* (Vol. XIV, Number 2), Fall 2004.